# F·I·T·N·E·S·S
## THE·Y's·WAY

by William B. Zuti, Ph.D.
edited by John H. Saxtan

YMCA of the USA

ISBN 0-88035-009-1

© National Board of Young Men's Christian Associations 1983

Available from:
  YMCA of the USA
  Program Resources
  6400 Shafer Court
  Rosemont, Illinois 60018
  (312) 228-7272

# F·I·T·N·E·S·S
## THE·Y's·WAY

YMCA of the USA

# Dedication

*To Lawrence A. Golding, Ph.D.*
*Scholar, teacher, researcher,*
*YMCA volunteer, and friend*

# Foreword

The goal of being physically fit has increased greatly in popularity in the United States over the past 15 years. There has been a proliferation of nonprofit, as well as for profit, health and fitness spas and centers throughout the country. In addition, there has been a proliferation of do-it-yourself materials including books, records, audiovisual materials, and even computerized systems.

While medical authorities agree that a reasonable level of physical and mental fitness is essential for a life of quality, authorities are not unanimous in recommending any single method for attaining such physical and mental fitness. All of our citizens do not recognize the beneficial effect of a "sound mind in a healthy body" in reducing the probability of developing disease, disability, or death. Moreover, many of our citizens do not know what constitutes an appropriate level of fitness or how such fitness can be achieved. Many of the materials on the market today focus on achieving quick results with minimal or no effort. Such means of obtaining fitness frequently focus on a single specific type of activity such as running, dancing, jogging, weight lifting, or one or another obscure diet.

This book, sponsored by the YMCA, provides the essential information that all individuals should know about becoming and staying physically fit. It is written in language easily understood by anyone of high school age and competence. It will be a value to all who are interested in fitness, whether they have engaged in their own fitness programs for years or are just beginning their first class at the YMCA or other fitness center.

Its contents represent a reasonable and valuable presentation of the how and why of physical fitness for individuals of all ages.

Jesse L. Steinfeld, M.D., Dean
School of Medicine
Medical College of Virginia/VCU
(Former U.S. Surgeon General)

# Acknowledgement

Some of the material in this book is based on *The Y's Way to Physical Fitness: A Guidebook for Instructors.* That text, assembled by a national team of expert volunteers and edited by Lawrence A. Golding, Ph.D., Clayton R. Myers, Ph.D., and Wayne E. Sinning, Ph.D., is now in its second edition and recognized as an authoritative book on physical fitness. We believe it is only right to acknowledge the importance of that text which was so helpful and made this non-instructor's guide possible and as complete as it is.

Bill Zuti

# Contents

# Introduction

Another book on physical fitness, you ask? Yes, but we certainly hope not an ordinary one. Most of the physical fitness books available today are specifically aimed at men, or women, or runners, or weight lifters, and so on. Many fitness books concentrate on weight loss or spot reducing through special diets and exercise. To attract readers they promise amazing results in 10 days or 10 weeks. When readers fail to achieve the promised results, they get discouraged and abandon the entire program. Well, this book is written for the typical person who wants to achieve and maintain overall fitness. It promises no quick-loss diets, no Herculean muscle plans, and no 10-day wonders. It does promise to provide you with the information you need to make intelligent choices in exercising, dieting, and living patterns which will help you on your way to physical fitness.

Who will benefit from this book? People mature enough to make the commitment to fitness for the rest of their lives, which means just about everybody of high school age or older. No special considerations are needed for any age group or occupation, because the principles stated here apply to all. While specific types of activities may vary with age or even as a person moves from one area of the country to another, the principles of fitness remain the same.

It is very important that you be in good general health to use this book. You should have been pronounced healthy by a physician within the past year. If you are very overweight, over 40 and smoke heavily, or have a family history of heart disease or other illnesses, check with your doctor before engaging in any fitness program and please read Chapter 3 and the section on Risk Factors.

There is a great deal of discussion these days about "wellness." This fitness book deals in many ways with the wellness concept of living. Wellness is an individual commitment to a pattern of living that promotes overall health and minimizes illness. Wellness is not just physical fitness, but includes emotional and spiritual wellbeing. Eating right, getting enough exercise, drinking moderately or not at all, and avoiding smoking and drugs are all aspects of wellness. Community service, ethical behavior, and a positive management of stress-inducing situations are also included in total wellness. These areas are all interrelated, so people who have made fitness their goal are well on the way to a wellness lifestyle. You will find many of these interrelationships mentioned in this book.

# How To Use This Book

Every effort has been made to keep this book as non-technical as possible. You do not have to know anything about exercise, diet, equipment, or other programs to be able to understand what is said here. The first five chapters explain all about exercise, how it affects your body, how it affects your lifestyle, and how you can find out what shape you are in now so you know where to begin. The following chapters outline how to establish a program which is best suited to you. The last chapter is a listing of resource material which you may use to find more information on general and specific areas of fitness.

We recommend that you read through the book entirely before beginning your program. That will give you an overall idea of the logical progression of the chapters and answer many of the questions you may ask during the reading. We hope you enjoy it and we welcome you to a lifetime of fitness.

# 1. Benefits of Fitness

Fitness benefits a person primarily in two primary ways: physically and emotionally. The physical benefit allows you to do more things, do them well, and do them for a longer period of time. Like the proverbial well-oiled machine, a fit body has greater potential than a rusty one. A person whose body is well conditioned has good stamina and can keep at an activity without becoming too tired too soon. New activities can be learned thanks to this new-found stamina, which allows one to practice and master new skills. Also, a well-toned body is less likely to suffer injury from the rigors of daily living or new activities.

It is believed that fit people recover faster from illness and surgery than less fit people although there hasn't been much research in this area. Many corporations today are taking a look at the theory that sponsoring a fitness program helps reduce absenteeism and increases production. The results are encouraging, but not yet conclusive.

On the proven and realistic side, you may not be interested in running the Boston Marathon or entering a body-building contest, but you should be interested in being able to cut the grass without being tired for the rest of the weekend, and be interested in having the stamina to take up tennis or some other activity.

Emotionally, fitness can contribute a great deal to your own self-image. Most people will agree that physically fit people tend to be judged more attractive than less fit people. The better you look the better you feel; self-confidence increases and you get along better with others. An added plus is that clothes may fit more comfortably and you will generally have a wider selection. Designers, famous or otherwise, tend to make clothes for the fitter frame. Fitness activities can also contribute to your social life. As your activities and interests increase, you will find more to talk about, meet new people who share similar interests, and probably encourage your friends to join you in your new patterns of living.

Stress is a big problem in daily life, and fitness activities provide a release for stress. Vigorous activity vents the frustrations of the day, loosens tight muscles, and can help you cope with the stress-causing problems. You can strike back at a source of frustration with a racquet or broom—a vigorous game of tennis or an hour of brisk garage or house cleaning.

As you progress in your fitness program, you will probably seek out new activities as your interests and energy grow. These additions contribute to your overall enjoyment of life and emotional health by broadening your skills, your interests, and your acquaintances. If you are already fit and have hobby sports such as scuba diving, hang gliding, or skiing, a fitness program will keep you in shape to enjoy these sports more and allow you to continue them for a longer time.

# 2. The Commitment

Some people think of fitness the way they think of painting a room—once it's done they can forget about it until it's needed again. It just isn't so. Fitness requires not only an immediate short-term commitment to get into shape, but also a long-term, lifetime commitment to keep in shape. If you are a beginner at fitness or you are very far out of shape, you may not like doing all that has to be done at the beginning. You'll have to keep reminding yourself that the things that are best for you are often uncomfortable at first. Fitness is an aquired taste and you will learn to wonder how you ever did without it.

Fortunately, there are many ways to make exercise more fun. If you are taking part in an organized class such as aerobic dancing or exercise class, the instructors will do all they can to make it fun. Plus you will meet interesting new people. Do yourself a favor and take a friend along and share your adjustment pangs and fun. Let yourself get out of cutting the grass or washing the dishes so you can go to class. Yes, you'll still have to do those things later, but there's an added pleasure to things you do when you play hookey.

As you own fitness program grows, not all your activities will be in organized groups. To keep up your interest, vary your routine. If you bicycle for exerise, pedal through different neighborhoods or buy a basket for your bike and give up driving to the store.

Fitness will eventually become a way of life for you, physically and emotionally. Admittedly, it is a major adjustment and it will take about one year before you are really comfortable with the new life-style. (Yes, a whole 12 months). This is why personal commitment is so important. Instead of thinking of fitness in terms of painting a room, think of it as re-doing a 12-room house; each month you finish one room and progress to the next. At the end of one year the whole house is done, but now you have to main-tain it—which is easier than redoing it, but still re-quires a regular effort and commitment.

One of the best ways to maintain your momentum and keep up your commitment is to find a partner. This can be a friend or neighbor or just someone else you've met who has similar fitness goals. Maybe you'll meet at an exercise class or when you are out jogging, but wherever you find one, a partner is a real key to success, especially for beginners. The reason for a partner is that you will each encourage the other. And by feeling responsible to the other party you will show up when you don't really feel like it and so will your partner. You keep each other going in spite of yourselves. This is the buddy system.

If you can't find a partner, use the support of a whole group such as an exercise class at your YMCA. Just make sure the group comes close to matching you in abilities and interests and that the group as a whole is as committed as you are or want to be.

Before you get the idea that the only route to success is through organized exercise classes, it should be re-emphasized that there is a broad range of activities from which to choose, organized and informal. If you have been relatively sedentary and eating poorly, but are in good general health, any increase in exercise or quality of diet is bound to be an improvement for you. Chapter Nine in this book lists over a dozen common activities and their benefits, so choose the ones you like to do best. It makes the commitment easier.

## Goal Setting

Fitness is not an overnight project, it is a long-term commitment. You have to be realistic in your expectations. Learn where you are now and establish where you eventually want to be. Establish goals to meet along the way. Goals should be quantifiable, for example, in pounds, inches, distance or time, and should be set to bring a realistic improvement by a specific time. An example would be if you were currently doing 20 sit-ups in three minutes, to try to raise that to 25 sit-ups within three minutes (consistently) by the end of the next two weeks. The most realistic approach is to establish short-term and long-term goals.

Short-term goals, if realistic, will help you see progress quickly on your long road to overall fitness. Such goals might take the form of losing five pounds, or shortening the time you run a certain distance.

Long-term goals will vary with your ultimate objectives and expectations. If you want to be a distance runner, your long-term goal may be to compete in a 10-kilometer run. To achieve that you need to set intermediate goals which will lead up to it. Overall, your ultimate long-term goal should be to achieve an increase in fitness and health. You may simply want to achieve a state of wellbeing in which you can do all the gardening you want without becoming exhausted, or maybe you want to look trim in slacks with a smaller waist. Whatever your ultimate long-term goal, it can only be achieved by successfully establishing and meeting short-term goals which mark your progress and spur you on to the next steps.

One of the greatest pitfalls of people setting out to establish a healthier mode of living is that they expect to accomplish too much too soon. Let's take an extreme example: Joe is 45 years old, smokes two packs of cigarettes a day, pays little attention to what he eats, drinks a little too much, and doesn't get enough exercise, so he's overweight as well. His job is stressful, which is why he smokes and drinks, and he never seems to have any time for his family.

Joe re-examines his life and decides to adopt a

wellness attitude and change his life for the better. So he takes the plunge. All at once he goes on a diet, tries to stop drinking and smoking, plans family activities, and signs up for a course in stress management.

Chances are Joe will fail in all of these things. He is trying to do too much at one time. He would be much better off if he did only a few things at once or even one at a time. He could sign up for a stress management course and try to quit smoking at the same time because the two are related.

Trying to change everything at once is just too much for most people. Joe will most likely become discouraged about his progress on one goal and end up giving them all up as fruitless. The point is that it is better to take one thing at a time and progress in short steps to the realization of that goal. And then, when progress is being made and you feel good about it, another area can be added.

Just as you should not try to do everything at once, you must make your goals very realistic and again not expect too much too soon. You can't expect to lose 25 pounds in one week, at least not safely. But you could realistically expect to lose two or three pounds. It took you longer than you probably realize to gain the 25 pounds you want to lose, so it is going to take a while to get rid of them, too.

## Self-Appraisal

Each of us is our own worst critic, so you have to relearn how to be your own best friend. If you set realistic, measurable goals, the facts of your progress will speak for themselves. Don't get too discouraged if you backslide a little bit. Backsliding happens to everyone. Typically you just can't pass up the cake at someone's wedding, or you have to take a customer out for a fancy dinner and it will blow your whole diet plan for a while. Don't quit just because you aren't 100 percent perfect all the time. Learn to think of all the times you were good about your diet or your exercise program and remember the progress you've made so far. One step backward doesn't erase all the steps you've made forward.

Sailing offers a good analogy. To reach a port (your goal) in sailing, you may have to tack back and forth across the unfavorable wind to make headway. The port is always there as a goal, but, unless the winds are continually in your favor, the direction you take to reach that port is not a straight line. Your personal fitness goal is out there in front of you—you set it—and there are many winds against you. To reach the goal you may have to try different ways to make things work for you, but if you keep your goal in mind, eventually you will make it.

## Personal Considerations

We all have our own reasons for wanting fitness, and we have our own ways of achieving it. As said earlier, fitness takes effort and a commitment to keep working at it. It is important that you examine your own commitment to fitness in light of your own personal considerations.

First, look at yourself and your current level of

fitness. You should be able to analyze realistically where you are, where you want to be, and how large the gap is. The larger the gap, the longer the timetable to reach your anticipated goal. But don't get discouraged just because the gap is large. Remember your short-term goals which will mark your progress and keep you going.

Next, review your current patterns of living. Are you a smoker? A heavy drinker? A person who gets little exercise and eats haphazardly? How much are you willing to change to start?

You don't have to (and shouldn't) change everything all at once, but you must be prepared to make some changes now and others later. Obviously your current mode of living didn't get you into a state of supreme fitness or you wouldn't be reading this book. So ask yourself what and how much you are willing to change. Once you have the answers, you can be realistic about starting a personal program and setting goals.

Finding time for exercising is probably the most difficult thing to overcome for beginners. "Not having any time" is probably the number one excuse for not starting a program, so let's just assume you can find the time if you really want to.

There is no ideal time to exercise. Some people enjoy it more in the morning and others enjoy it more at night. Since we are only talking about an hour or so, you can readily see how some people fit the exercise portion of fitness into their lunch hours or immediately before or after work. You should experiment with different times, but try to find one time that works out best for you on a regular basis. Establishing a routine is important. It makes exercise a regular part of your day, just like other events in your schedule—church, meals, or your favorite television program. You want it to be so regular that you feel that something is missing if you get off schedule.

Another consideration is the type of facilities needed to perform whatever activities you have chosen. If you think you would enjoy swimming as part of your fitness routine, do you have easy access to a pool? If the nearest pool is 25 miles away and you hate driving there because there is never any place to park, you're defeating yourself from the start. Many activities need only limited space or equipment to perform, so you should again choose those that will fit in easily with your daily schedule and plans.

Equipment, even if you choose jogging, is something else to be considered. Buy good equipment, but only purchase what you really need. Avoid gadgetry such as "sauna suits" or designer sweat bands. A good program doesn't need any large outlay of money to be effective. If you join a fitness center or other facility, compare the equipment and programs with others nearby before you sign up. What you really need is access to their facilities and the program, not fancy lighting fixtures, so make sure that you will have access to the equipment you need at the times you want. Some clubs alternate men's and women's sessions or limit usage times of equipment.

Make sure the rules fit your commitment of time.

No matter how organized a program you join, the commitment and considerations are still very personally yours. If you examine a program carefully, evaluate your personal life, and see how the two will fit together, you are more likely to succeed in your endeavor and to receive the full enjoyment and benefit from it.

# 3. Understanding Your Body

To appreciate fully the effects of fitness, or non-fitness, on your body, it is important to understand certain basic information about how the body is composed and how its various systems work. This is not a textbook chapter on physiology, so don't turn the pages too quickly to get to the "good" stuff later on in this book.

Obviously, when we speak of fitness we are referring to the body and its functions. Any knowledge you can acquire toward understanding your body will enable you to make more intelligent decisions about your individual program of health and fitness.

One of the main points you should gain from this chapter, even if you don't remember very much about the separate body systems, is that the workings of the whole is dependent on the parts. The body is the ultimate example of synergism, or the interrelationship of distinct components. The muscles are affected by the cardiovascular system; the metabolic rate is affected by the body's oxygen usage; your appearance is affected by the fat accumulation which is affected by body structure, diet, and metabolism; so on. Even though you can concentrate your efforts on one area of the body, you will still be affecting other parts. This is good. If you had to do separate exercise and diets for each area, you would probably end up exhausted and with little time to do anything else. So, keep in mind the synergism of the body and understand the interrelations of the systems.

## Body Composition

Body composition, also called body type, is really a result of inheritance. While you may not have the body type of your parents (even if you may strongly resemble one), your body type is a combination of their genes to create your composition. Given the choice, many of us would have chosen the long, lean, muscular body type that is favored by American society today. Few of us are fortunate enough to be that type, and none of us had a choice in the matter. While a lucky few have the desired body type, even fewer still fall into the category known as the gifted athlete.

There is nothing that can be done to change your body type, not even major surgery, so the important thing is to do the most with what you've got. Fortunately, fitness is not dependent on body type. While your ultimate potential in sports or even your ability to look good in certain types of clothes may be limited, you can still achieve fitness and your *maximum potential* for physical development.

It is important that you do not get overly concerned about adopting a goal that is completely unrealistic for your body type. A simple example is Jane Fonda and Dolly Parton, both attractive entertainers, but with completely different body types. Neither could look like the other no matter what she might do. And most people would agree that they have each done the most with what they have. If you have short, stocky stature, you cannot realistically expect to exercise and diet and become a Jane Fonda. And the same applies to men as well, with their equivalent examples.

Fat is usually the major concern of someone trying to achieve fitness and an attractive appearance. We need fat for several reasons. Fat provides physical protection; it acts as a bumper between the body and the outside world. Fat provides insulation and helps keep the body warmer than it would be if there were no layer of fat. Fat also provides an "emergency" energy reserve which the body can call upon in stress and keep going without having a collapse of its systems. And finally, fat is essential to appearance. If the skin were stretched over the muscles and bones without a layer of fat in between, the resulting appearance would be bumpy and unattractive. Fat provides the smooth contours that give the body its appealing appearance.

Historically, meaning thousands of years ago, fat was necessary for food storage to get a person through periods of famine. Other animals still use fat in this way. Humans have advanced beyond this survival need for fat.

Controlling the amount of accumulated fat on the body is important. Not only is too much unattractive, but it can be detrimental to your health. Note that the emphasis is on controlling "overfat" rather than "overweight"—the difference is important. Being overweight means exceeding the established norms for a height and body type. These norms are simply averages and can be very misleading. A very muscular body builder can be very overweight according to the norms, yet have very little fat on his body. Conversely, a person can fall within the norms and still have an excess accumulation of fat, because the muscle buildup is so lacking in proportion. Chapter Six explains in greater detail how the percent of fat is determined for an individual.

Theoretically, losing excess fat is simple; you just expend more calories than you take in and eventually the excess fat will disappear. Like most theories, it is easier said than done. And this is not accomplished by will power alone. It is a complex process.

The two ways you can use up more calories than you take in are eating fewer calories and expending more energy, usually through exercise. There are literally thousands of low-calorie diet plans around today. In the short run many of them are effective, but in the long run most of them are not. The problem is that people tend to use a low-calorie diet plan for only a short time, until they have lost the weight they wanted to lose. Then they return to their old eating habits. The only sensible long-term eating plan which will be effective is a change in eating habits. It is hard to change habits, but it can be done. And there are some surprisingly simple things you can do to reduce your eating. Of course, at the same time you need to plan what you eat.

First, serve away from the table. If you put platters and bowls on the table and let everyone help themselves, the visual signal that there is more food available will encourage excessive eating. Secondly, if you use slightly smaller plates or bowls when serving, the portions will look larger. It's all in your head, but it works. Next, don't leave food out where it can be seen or store it in see-through containers in the refrigerator. Just as serving at the table tempts you visually, so does food stored so you can see it. Finally, set a routine for meals: same times, same places. Concentrate on enjoying the food and not on something else which can distract you from how much you are eating. Sitting in front of the TV is an excellent way to overeat, because you eat almost mindlessly and ignore the food.

You can't "break" a habit, you can only change it. So if adults set a good example for today's children (while they may have to suffer through changes), the correct habits will be established for the next generation.

A last word on eating concerns "cleaning your plate." Depending on your age you were probably told to "remember the starving children in Europe" or to waste not, want not, as an encouragement to finishing everything on your plate. This is where a bad habit was started. There's a saying, better to waste food than to have food go to your waist. The food is already paid for, eating it won't get the money back. In the long run it really is better to waste it than to waist it.

## The Muscular/Skeletal System

The muscular/skeletal system is made up of three components: muscles, connective tissue, and bone. Muscles provide the power. They pull against the connective tissue. Connective tissue, the most important being the tendons, connects the muscles to the bones. The bones are the levers. This is the way we move or work.

The major qualities of the muscular/skeletal system are strength, endurance, and flexibility.

Strength can be measured as the single most forceful contraction of a muscle you can generate.

Endurance can be divided into absolute and relative. Absolute endurance is measured by seeing how many repetitions you can do with a fixed benchmark weight. Relative endurance measures the number of repetitions which can be done with a weight proportional to your strength.

Absolute endurance relates directly to strength, whereas relative endurance is a function of training. For example, let us take a man and a woman. To figure strength, each would find the maximum weight with which he or she can do one repetition of the exercise.

Let us say the man can use 50 lbs., the woman 25.

The man is stronger. To figure absolute endurance, give them the same weight (say 25 lbs.) for the exercise. The man will be able to do several repetitions, the woman one. The man has greater absolute endurance because he is stronger. To figure relative endurance, give them each 50% of their maximum weight. For this the man would have 25 lbs., the woman, 12.5. The woman might be able to do 10, while the man can only do five, because this test reflects endurance training. Relative endurance is used in training because using strength, with the exception of the muscle groups of the hands, poses too great a chance of injury. Strength is then estimated and strength is measured using endurance.

Flexibility is moving a joint through its full range of motion. This movement is limited by three things: the skeletal system, which limits how far a joint can move; the ability to elongate a muscle; and the length, or distension, of the connective tissue. With the exception of skeletal limitations, training can increase flexibility.

Muscles are the prime movers of your body; they get you where you want to go and let you do what you want to do, such as walk across a room and open a door. Muscles also affect metabolism (the rate of energy expenditure) since it is the muscles which use the calories. Muscles affect your appearance according to their firmness or tone. Muscles which are not properly exercised even without excess fat will lack tone and firmness and this will show through.

When the muscular/skeletal system is exercised, it

is important to balance the exercises so that the extenders and the flexors are equally trained. These muscles do what their names say. The triceps are an extender muscle you use to straighten out your arm, while the biceps are the flexor to bend it back. If not equally trained, you will look unbalanced, plus you greatly increase the possibility of injury.

The advantage of good muscular conditioning is that it allows you to do the exercises for cardiovascular training, burns up the calories to limit fat accumulation, and increases your flexibility. Again, the idea of synergism coming through.

## The Cardiovascular System

The heart and lungs, with their associated components, comprise the two major features of the cardiovascular system. They work together to oxygenate the blood and pump it coursing through our blood vessels.

The bloodstream carries nutrients and oxygen to the cells. They use the nutrients and oxygen, then the waste products, such as carbon dioxide and heat, are carried away in the bloodstream to be expelled from the body in a variety of ways. If a cell doesn't get enough food and oxygen, or the excrement can't be released, the cell can't function properly.

Oxygen is critical for cell life. If a cell goes without oxygen for more than a few minutes, it is in extreme danger of dying. Blood carried through the arteries is the primary source of oxygen for cell life. In an unhealthy body, cholesterol and other fats may build up in the arteries and block the flow of blood, and therefore oxygen, to the cells. A blocked artery in the heart or brain can be extremely serious and cause permanent injury and sometimes death. Physical conditioning can help maintain the C-V system.

The heart muscle is similar to the skeletal muscles in its response to exercise. Exercising the heart by causing it to pump harder increases the force of the contractions, which eventually makes the heart a better, more efficient pump. With training, the heart will empty more completely, pump at a lower rate, and it can rest longer between strokes while still delivering more blood to the body. In short, it does a better job with less work.

Initially, exercise participants will experience an increased heart rate as they exercise since the heart is not yet conditioned. Over time, the heart rate will not increase as much when exercising at this same pace because it has become conditioned. To condition the heart a fit person must then increase his or her work load accordingly.

*Blood Pressure*

One of the things that moves the blood through the vessels is pressure. Blood pressure, which is reported in numeric values for the "systolic" and "diastolic" pressures is usually written systolic/diastolic. Systolic pressure is the pumping pressure of the heart. The diastolic pressure is the pressure which remains in the body when the heart is not pumping.

When the diastolic pressure becomes excessively high, the heart has to work against it. This means the heart has to work harder, which causes more wear and tear on the heart and the blood vessels. Also, excessively high pressure tends to rupture small blood vessels. This can be minor and possibly even go unnoticed if it happens in some areas of the body. But if the rupture occurs in a vital area such as the brain (this is what is called a stroke), major damage and disability can result.

Your blood pressure and heart rate fluctuate readily as you become excited or as you exercise. The systolic pressure, however, is the pressure which changes the most. A person with a resting blood pressure of 120/80 may find that the pressure has even risen to 160/85 after exercise. Sometimes the diastolic pressure even drops a little after exercise.

High blood pressure, known as hypertension, is of great concern because of the damaging affects that can result. Fortunately, it is very easily checked by trained professionals and volunteers. And today there are frequent free blood pressure checks sponsored by organizations as a community service. It is known that hypertension can be hereditary and that it occurs more frequently among blacks. It is important for you to learn if you have hypertension.

Anyone with hypertension should seek the advice of a physician. Some people will be helped by decreasing salt intake, reducing excess weight, and a planned program of regular exercise.

*Heart Rate*
Heart rate is dependent on the demands of the body. It is controlled by the automatic systems of the body

body and there is little we can do to control the heart rate, unlike control of skeletal muscles or even breathing. Other than excitement, the major cause of increased heart rate is a build-up of waste products in the cells. When excitement occurs, the heart rate increases to ready the body for "fight or flight." In the same way it increases to the level needed to carry off waste products from the cells when increased activity, such as exercise, occurs.

The cardiovascular system is affected by training, becoming more efficient in carrying oxygen to the cells and in carrying off the waste products produced. Workload capacity is increased because the body is supplied with the oxygen and other substances that it needs to continue whatever activity you are doing. This makes awareness of the cardiovascular system extremely important in any training program.

*Metabolism*

Metabolism is the process by which food is burned to produce energy. Energy is needed to do work. We also need to burn the foodstuffs coming in to avoid the accumulation of fat.

Breathing supplies the oxygen you need for the majority of the body's metabolism. Fortunately, breathing is an automatic response, so you don't have to learn how to do it. True, you can control your breathing to a large extent, but there really is no reason to learn any special way of breathing for exercising. It doesn't matter whether you breathe in or out through your nose or mouth; simply do what comes most naturally. Of course, the mouth is much larger than the nose, so during heavy exercise it is easier to breathe through the mouth. Also, during heavy exercise you will tend to use the rib cage as well as the diaphragm to move air in and out of the lungs. Beginners may feel difficulty in breathing and even experience some chest discomfort. Within a short time and with training, this breathing becomes easier. If discomfort is severe or persistant, see a physician.

The oxygen in the air you breathe is transferred to the blood which carries it to the cells of the body. The cells give up carbon dioxide (waste) and take the oxygen. The cells then use the oxygen to burn the fuel to produce energy. Humans produce their most efficient energy aerobically, that is, with oxygen. Some energy can be produced without oxygen, but it isn't very efficient and it does require oxygen later on to pay back what is called the "oxygen debt" to the body.

In exercise, we look at energy units in two ways. First, there is the amount of oxygen needed to do a certain amount of work. This is called the oxygen uptake. The other energy unit is the calorie. A calorie is the amount of heat needed to raise one gram of water from 19 to 20 degrees Celsius. The kilocalorie is in common usage. This is the amount of heat required to raise 1000 grams of water one degree Centigrade. A soft drink which lists 100 calories on its label actually means 100 kilocalories. This is the measurement used for most foods. For the purposes of this book we will use "calorie" to mean kilocalorie, sometimes abbreviated as a capital "C".

A pound of body fat contains 3,500 calories, which is the amount of energy it has stored. When one liter of oxygen is burned, it will produce approximately five calories of heat. So, to burn off a pound of body fat you would have to do activity enough to burn approximately 700 liters of oxygen. As an example of what that might take, a runner can use about two liters of oxygen per minute. So a runner would have to jog for almost six hours to burn off a pound of fat.

In learning about training, and in talking with others, you may hear a relatively new term used: the MET. It is simply the first three letters of metabolism and is used as a basic reference unit without figuring out the oxygen uptake, etc., of each separate activity. One MET is your resting metabolism. That is when you are asleep. Daily activities can then be expressed in multiples of your resting metabolism and give you some idea of how much work you are doing. Standing might translate to 2 METs, while walking might be 3 METs. Mets can be expressed in terms of oxygen uptake, but how this is figured is of more interest to scientists than people in training.

## Diet

Diet is a word which is often misused in America. In reality it means whatever you normally consume. You could, for instance, be on a diet of chocolate ice cream and beer if that were your normal food pattern. It's not a recommended diet, but it is a diet. Through popular usage, diet is usually associated with a low-calorie or low-fat pattern of eating, but again this is only a narrow interpretation. In this book, diet will be used to mean a well-balanced pattern of eating which provides the daily essential nutrients to the body without causing excessive fat accumulation. You can eat too much of the right things.

A proper diet provides the essential building blocks of the body. People can be physically fit, training to their utmost, and yet still not be as healthy as they could be, if they are not eating right and getting the essential nutrients daily. Just as nutritious eating habits alone will not make you physically fit, neither will physical conditioning make up for poor eating habits.

"Junk food" is a popular term today, applied most frequently to fast-food. There really is no such thing as "junk" food, because it all has some nutritional value. It is just that some food has more nutritional values than others. Better we say some people have junky food habits, rather than they eat junk food. Certainly we all enjoy a piece of candy or fast-foods now or then. And that is fine as long as we recognize its limited food value and do not use it as a mainstay of our diet.

To keep your body at its healthiest, it is critical that you obtain all the essential nutrients daily. Many Americans' eating habits are not very good. Protein is very necessary, but many Americans eat too much and rely too heavily on meat for protein. Americans also tend to eat too much fat in all its various forms, and not eat enough complex carbohydrates such as fruits, vegetables, and grains. Simple sugars are carbohydrates, but Americans should get away from them and eat more complex carbohydrate foods. Fiber, which years ago was more common in American diets, is again gaining favor from nutritionists. The fiber content of our diets can be wisely increased. Also, processing foods often adds things, like sugar, which we don't need more of and takes away many of the nutrients of which we do need more. The closer a food we eat is to the way it was grown, the more nutrition we are likely to get out of it.

## Fluids

Fluid intake is another critical area of diet. Basically, most people just don't drink enough water. They drink just about everything but water, such as soda pop or beer. In many instances this is becoming ridiculous as marketers reduce these beverages to flavored water by taking out the calories, caffeine, etc. Not so surprisingly, in some social circles water has become the "in" thing to drink for whatever reasons. At least this is one good food fad. Natural water is the perfect replacement for the water the body loses each day through sweat and excrement.

During exercise it is important to maintain fluid levels by drinking a pint of water for every pound of weight loss during exercise, as well as maintaining a regular intake of two to four pints of water each day through eating and drinking. The weight loss you may experience immediately after exercising is really water loss, not fat loss. You want to replace the water you lose to keep your body fluids in balance. With a proper diet, your body will eliminate any excess water, so you don't have to worry that you are adding any real weight by drinking water after exercising.

Diet and nutrition is a broad area that deserves more detailed attention from you than can be covered in this book. There are excellent courses available through local YMCAs and other organizations, and numerous publications on the subject. At the root of it all is the need to change your eating habits if you are not now following a healthy regimen. In many ways the saying, you are what you eat, holds a great deal of truth.

You should know about a number of other factors about your body and how these factors might affect a training program. Two primary ones, age and environment, are discussed here.

# Age

Age can be viewed in two ways, either chronologically, i.e., how many years old you are, or physiologically, which compares your body condition against a norm of some kind. Physiological comparisons are not easy because some 20-year-olds can't do what some 40-year-olds can. However, physiological aspects are what should govern what a person does or does not do when undertaking an exercise program.

Unfortunately there is no easy way to determine physiological age, so the tendency is to suggest strongly that anyone over 40 have a physical screening prior to entering a fitness program. This is usually good advice, but too many people think that they are the exception to the rule and don't bother with a physical. The fact of the matter is that 10 or 20 years does affect what you can do, no matter what you think, and the chances of injury are greatly increased by taking on too much to start. Again, you must be realistic in your program.

Some physiologists believe that peak physical performance is reached around the mid-20's. After that, ability and endurance decline. However, many aspects of physiological age can be prolonged by maintaining fitness. Depending on your beginning condition, you could work up to a high level of fitness and, through continued exercise, maintain a plateau so that the decline is much less rapid.

For those who are already past their peak, and physiologically older than they are chronologically (in other words, out of shape), fitness training can actually reverse the decline, establishing their own plateau. Naturally, it is easier to start early in life and maintain fitness, but a late start is still profitable. The body is slower to recoup as it gets older and the maximum heart rate slows with age.

# Environment

Environmental considerations for fitness training include heat, humidity, cold, and altitude.

## Heat

One of the problems of exercising in heat is that the same body system which delivers the oxygen to the cells also is responsible for cooling the body. When the body is very hot, the blood is moved near the surface of the skin to help cool the body and thereby is shunted away from the muscles which need the oxygen. This can cause a heat stress situation. Blood taken away from the muscles definitely affects your performance in heat.

Evaporation is one way the body gets cooled off and this is done by sweating. Surprisingly, some people really don't sweat, or don't sweat well, and this makes them very uncomfortable in hot weather and can limit their exercise routine. Because sweat is an efficient way to cool the body, the better trained an individual is, the more easily and more quickly he or she will sweat. It becomes a conditioned response. Of course, there is a great range of sweat rates for the population as a whole. Humidity must also be considered. The higher the relative humidity, the more slowly sweat will evaporate. So you won't cool effectively.

Another way the body is cooled is through convection: air currents (such as wind) moving across the exposed skin. Radiation and conduction are other ways the body is cooled, but these are relatively minor.

When exercising in heat it is useful to expose as much skin surface to the air as possible. This will aid evaporation and convection cooling. If rules or modesty limit the amount of skin you can expose, wear thin layers of clothes that will wet easily and cling to the skin to achieve the same effect. If you are in bright sunshine, you should protect yourself by wearing light colors which reflect the rays more than dark colors.

In excessive heat, plan to do your exercising in the cooler, early morning hours or inside.

*Cold*

Actually, very few people exercise in a cold environment, despite the advantage that your metabolism provides you with a ready source of heat. Actually, the ideal temperature range for strenuous exercise is 40 to 60 degrees Farenheit. If you do exercise in temperatures this cool, start by being dressed warmly, with a sweater or a jacket on, and then remove the layers as your body warms up.

Extreme cold can be dangerous due to the hazard of frostbite, but there is actually very little danger of freezing your lungs.

*Altitude*

Altitude is of minor concern to most people for exercise, but may be of more concern for occasional recreational sports such as skiing. The higher the altitude, the thinner the air and the less oxygen the blood will be able to absorb from your breathing. The answer is to moderate your exercise until you become adjusted. People who live in high-altitude regions such as Denver automatically adjust to the long-term exposure to thin air and their exercise programs would be no different than someone else's at a lower altitude.

## Summary

Understanding your body (and how training affects it) is important to deriving the most from any fitness program. Your body is made up of a complex interaction of systems and you must exercise each of these to reach your maximum potential. Diet plays a critical part in your body's fitness and should not be overlooked just because you are exercising and feeling good about it. The most important reminder is that you should determine what shape you are in and then proceed carefully toward your goal.

# 4. Principles of Exercising and Training

To get the most out of an exercise and training routine, it helps to know not only what to do, but how and why an exercise works. There are certain principles of exercise and training which, when understood, will lead you to getting the maximum effectiveness from your program. It also helps to know what *not* to do, and why, so the last part of this chapter gives the "nots" equal time. Some of these principles may seem obvious at first, but they will answer the questions you will no doubt have during your program and help you along your path to fitness.

## Overload

Overload is the principle of increasing the workload of an exercise. When you start your program you should start with a regimen which is relatively easy to accomplish. As your body adjusts to this workload, you overload it. If you are jogging, you may run a little farther or a little faster, in a repetitious exercise you add repetitions. When the body adjusts to the increased workload, you increase it again.

Highly trained athletes use the principle of maximum overload to increase the training effect. This is particularly effective in weight training when the muscle is purposely fatigued. A weight trainer who can do 10 repetitions with 100 pounds would first do 10 repetitions with 50 pounds, then 10 repetitions with 75 pounds, and finally try to do 10 repetitions with 100 pounds. This produces the maximum training effect.

Participants in a fitness program should not be concerned with maximum overload because, as noted above, it is for highly trained athletes. Fitness participants should stick with small increases in their programs as they progress. This will produce the desired effect with smaller chance of injury.

## Specificity

The principle of specificity is that you have to exercise the specific area where you want specific results. Synergism only goes so far. That is to say, you won't get good leg development by exercising your arms.

That sounds obvious, doesn't it; but the principle is carried further. Let's say that you are an avid handball player and want to increase your running speed and stamina. While running and jogging long distances will help you overall, it won't specifically help your handball skills. What you should do is some long-distance running with some wind sprints and shuttle runs back and forth.

If you want to develop a certain area, you must use it in practice the way you intend to use it elsewhere. Now, this usually applies more directly to athletics than it does to overall fitness, but if you have a specific goal in mind, remember this rule.

## All or None

The all-or-none law is helpful in understanding how your muscles work when you are training: When you flex a muscle, you control what happens by contracting a certain number of muscle fibers completely, not all of them partially. That is to say, if you use only half of your muscle power, you will use half of the fibers in complete contraction and half of them won't contract at all. You can't use only part of the fiber's contraction, since it contracts completely or not at all.

This is useful to know, because you might think that by working out partially you are exercising all your muscle fibers in whatever group you are training. In reality, you are only working part of those fibers, or part of that muscle. To get the most out of training a muscle you must exercise the entire muscle completely, which translates to hard work.

## Use and Dis-use

"Use it or lose it" is the more common way of expressing the use and dis-use principle, and it is true. The body is an extremely efficient machine and is constantly going through a self-evaluation process. What needs service, gets service. Those muscles which need the resources get all the resources; those that don't need it, don't get it. The extreme case of dis-use is atrophy, in which a muscle actually shrinks in size from lack of use. If you have ever been laid up in a hospital for several days, or had a broken limb, you know how quickly the limbs become weak from lack of use. They also recover quickly once you start using them again. So a well-balanced program of exercise will get you back into shape, even if you have an area which you have neglected.

## Train, Not Strain

Watch out for the following when you exercise. This is the list of "shalt not's". Now, the damage which you may be doing with these actions may not necessarily show up immediately or put you in severe pain, but a while later problems may show up. These actions can cause undue stress and possible injury so you are not doing an exercise correctly if you find yourself doing any of the following.

*Sporadic Exercise*

The sequence of body development is based on a consistent program of exercise. If you work out for two consecutive days, then skip three days, then exercise one day, then skip a week, you may be doing more harm than good.

As pointed out in an earlier chapter, the body builds up to levels of fitness through your exercise program and you have to keep challenging each new level to progress to the next. If you simply put the body through irregular stress periods, you aren't doing any good and you are subjecting the body to undue stress. Most training programs call for daily or every-other-day exercising. This keeps the progression going and, because the body is used to this level of exercise, you are not unduly stressing it. This is one of the things weekend athletes should be especially wary of. The opportunity for injury is greatly increased when there is no regular program of exercise to match the performance demands being made on it by irregular activity.

*Bouncing, Known as Ballistics*

The body does not respond well to sudden bouncing or jerking movements. Many people commit the error of thinking that they are stretching the muscles and increasing their flexibility when they "bounce" as they bend to touch their toes or do side bends. Actually, the reverse is true. When a muscle is suddenly jerked into a stretch, it responds by contracting. The classical example is the knee jerk response. Hitting the patella tendon with the doctor's rubber mallet causes a sudden stretching of that tendon. As a defense mechanism the muscle and tendon contract and the knee jerks.

So, if you bounce while doing an exercise you are actually causing the muscle fibers to contract, rather than stretch, and making the muscle work against itself. A torn muscle or torn tendon can be the result. Watch trained exercise instructors and you can see how fluid their movements are. There is no jerking or bouncing, just a smooth flow of action, even as they go from one exercise to another. If you find yourself bouncing, you are doing an exercise incorrectly and could do yourself some harm.

*Hyperextension of the Back*

Hyperextension of the back, or bending over backwards too far, is harmful because of the force placed on spine. The vertebrae just don't have that much space between them to accommodate this extreme flexion. A fractured or herniated disc (the cartilage between the vertebrae) could be the result. Some exercises do call for bending the back. The trouble comes when the back is overextended and put under pressure. Back bends would be one example, as would sitting on a Roman chair and bending as far back as you could and then pulling yourself up.

*Lateral Pressure to the Knee*

The lower leg is, by mechanical design, meant only to bend forward or back, not sideways. Any time you put lateral (sideways) pressure on the knee joint, you are asking for trouble.

*Pressure on the Neck*

The neck is not designed to bear a lot of weight or pressure. Puting too much pressure on it can obviously cause neck problems and pain. Head stands and lifting weights across the neck instead of the shoulders are typical examples.

*Excessive Weight Bearing*

Normal adults, meaning those not specially trained, should avoid lifting excessive weights whether it be a child or barbells. The rule of thumb is that men should limit themselves to lifting about 50 percent of their body weight and women limit themselves to about 35 percent.

These limits are based on average body muscle mass and not on any notions about "the weaker sex." The female has only 75 percent of the muscle mass of the male.

When lifting a heavy object, lift with the legs and not the back, avoid awkward positions, and try to carry the weight close to the center of the body. The main thing you want to avoid is overstraining the back, but since lifting a heavy weight in an awkward position could damage a knee, a leg, or an arm, always use caution.

# 5. Evaluation Testing/ Current State of Fitness

If someone asked you how to get to Chicago you would first want to know whether that person was in New York or Kansas City. So it is with fitness. You have to know where you are in order to determine how you go about getting where you want to be.

In some aspects you may be able to do a self-evaluation. Are you grossly overweight? You should be able to determine that for yourself. Do you think you tire too easily or your strength and endurance aren't what they should be? Do people think of you as older than you really are due to your appearance instead of your wisdom? These things reflect on your current state of fitness and can be subjectively judged by you. But the subjectivity is the problem.

As honest as people try to be about themselves, they end up being either too kind or too hard on themselves. The value of having a series of fitness evaluation tests is that they are objective. Also, fitness participants who haven't had a fitness evaluation are told to start at a very low level, such as walking, and work their way up. For many this may be the best way, but others may be able to start at a higher level and be able to progress toward their goals that much faster.

Without testing and without professional advice, an individual may start at too high a level of exercise and end up suffering injury and disappointment.

If you really want to know the honest facts (some may not be as bad as you imagined) and are serious about progressing to your goals, fitness evaluation testing is the way to go.

## Where to go for testing

There are opportunities for testing in many, if not most, communities. Almost every local YMCA offers a fitness evaluation, and many private organizations do, also. Looking in the Yellow Pages may help you find a place, or asking your doctor or the local school physical education teacher. Because of the danger of overstressing the body, cardiovascular testing is best done at a supervised facility under the guidance of a professional fitness specialist. Cost of a fitness evaluation test can vary greatly. The YMCA fitness center may include testing as part of its membership, while the Y and others may offer it as an independent testing, not tying it to any obligation to join or do anything with the results.

No matter where you go, there are some basic requirements for a proper evaluation.

First, a medical screening should be required from a physician which states that you are in good enough health to participate in a program of exercise (and the testing, of course).

Next, you should receive an informed consent form for you to sign, which tells the exact nature of the tests you will receive and what the meaning of those tests is.

Lastly, the test battery should include testing of cardiovascular fitness, some measure of body composition, some measure of strength and endurance, and an indication of flexibility. These are the four areas that comprise fitness, and they must be tested independently.

You can't have one test that does it all, or even a test that measures more than one of these areas at a time. If these four areas are not included in the testing you are considering, you will not be getting a complete fitness evaluation.

Now, some organizations may go beyond these four or have more in-depth testing in some areas, but these four areas must be measured to some extent to get any minimal evaluation. The tests and procedures used by the YMCA are standards for others and have been used and approved by experts, so testing at a local YMCA is highly recommended, though other agencies may be comparable.

The results of the tests will allow you to undertake a more individualized program, geared to your level of fitness. Chances are you will score well on some areas and not so well on others. This shows you where you really need to concentrate your efforts, while not neglecting others. For example, you might be carrying around more fat than you realize, even if you don't appear to be overweight. Your flexibility might be very good, but your strength and endurance are low. As a result, the tests will not only tell you what areas need work, but they can indicate what types of exercises you can do safely to improve those areas.

Pretesting tells you that you are in Kansas City and have to go east to get to Chicago. Without pretesting you could be in New York and still be told to go east. You'll reach Chicago eventually by going east from New York, but it's not the best way for you to get there.

## The Tests

The following sections give you an idea of the tests which you would take as part of a YMCA fitness evaluation. For each test listed here, we explain the method of administering it, the reason for taking it, and the meaning to you of the test. If you take any of these tests and you forget why you are taking it and what the results should mean to you, be sure to ask; the score of a test is just a bunch of useless information if you don't know what that means.

*Resting Heart Rate and Resting Blood Pressure*
These tests are usually the first two to be administered. As the test name implies, the body should be relatively rested and you should be at ease. These tests form the base line for other tests and therefore you should prepare yourself in minor ways. You should get a good night's rest, eat lightly, avoid caf-

feine or other stimulants and, if you smoke, you should not smoke for at least an hour before the test, preferably longer.

If you are on any medication which affects your heart rate, you should be certain that you have your doctor's okay for these tests and inform the tester. Because some of the other tests use your heart rate as an indication of the work load you can handle, any medication which keeps your heart rate low will result in you being given a work load which may exceed your safe capacity. Chances are that if you are under a doctor's care for any heart problems or other chronic illness, you should be in a specialized program and not one which is designed for the normally healthy individual.

For the resting heart rate test you will usually be asked to sit in a chair for five or more minutes and may be asked to fill out some forms to distract you and keep you relatively calm. The test is simply a counting of your pulse rate while you are at rest. Most people do very well on this, falling well within established norms. However, some individuals may have a very high resting heart rate and may be asked not to continue with the other tests.

The high resting heart rate may be due to nervousness or for some medical reason. A check by a physician is in order if your resting heart rate is in excess of 90 beats per minute (bpm). Most range from 50 to 70. A low resting rate is usually regarded as a good sign; it is an indication of an efficient cardiovascular system. However, resting heart rate is governed by hereditary factors, too.

Resting blood pressure is also taken after you have been seated in a chair for five or more minutes. You should sit relaxed, with both feet on the floor and not have your arms or legs crossed. Blood pressure is usually taken on the left arm, but either arm is okay.

Blood pressure varies considerably from one moment to the next, especially due to stress or activity, thus the reason for resting. Most individuals have an acceptable resting blood pressure, but again, if the pressure is too high, the individual will not be allowed to continue with the other tests until a physician has checked the reason. Normal range goes from 110/70 to 140/90.

Low blood pressure is seldom considered a problem unless the person experiences blackouts or other difficulties.

These tests are not diagnostic. All they tell you is that you fall (or don't fall) within normal ranges and therefore a normal fitness test can be assured. The tests just tell you what your heart rate and blood pressure are at that point in time, prior to testing.

The numbers in blood pressure readings, for example 120/80 (said as "one-twenty over eighty") are the pressures taken at two points during the test. The upper, higher number is called the systolic pressure. This is the pressure in the artery at that time, measured as the height in millimeters of a column of mercury that the artery would support if it were attached to it. This is the pumping pressure of the heart. The lower number is the diastolic pressure which is the resting, that is, passive, pressure of the artery.

Blood pressure is measured with a sphygmomanometer, the 16-letter name for a blood pressure cuff. Systolic pressure is measured as the air in the inflated cuff around your upper arm is slowly released. The cuff is pumped to the point that it exerts enough pressure to temporarily stop the flow of blood through the artery. As the pressure is released, a sound can be heard at the point at which the pumping heart is first able to overcome that pressure in the cuff and force blood through the artery again. The sound is caused by the vibration of the artery.

As the pressure in the cuff is reduced further, the vibration sound will eventually disappear at the point when the pressure in the cuff equals the pressure in the artery. This is the diastolic pressure reading.

High blood pressure, that which falls beyond the established norms, is a basis for concern because, as mentioned in Chapter Three, the heart and cardiovascular system have to work against this pressure and that can be detrimental. The likelihood of stroke and heart attack is also increased, so hypertension (high blood pressure) should be examined by a physician.

### Body Composition

Body composition tests are designed to determine if you are carrying around too much fat in relation to your "ideal" body size. They are not designed to tell you your hips are too big, or you are too short or tall, or that you have oversized feet. As mentioned in the opening chapter, your body shape, coloring, etc., are a result of heredity. There is little you can do to change the basic structure, but body composition tests can tell you if you are carrying too much fat proportionally for *your* body.

There are some very simple measures which you can conduct yourself to get a general idea if you have too much fat. One is to find the roll of fat (everyone has a little) at your belt line, just above your hips.

On either side, roll up this fat between two fingers of one hand and then place the index finger of the other hand over the roll between the holding fingers. If the roll is greater than this finger width, you are carrying too much fat. Although this is only a "quickie" way of measuring fat, it does have the advantage of taking into consideration body size, age, and sex differences automatically.

It bears repeating here what has been said before about the differences between being "overweight" and "overfat". While some people use the terms interchangeably, overweight means that weight exceeds established norms. A very muscular person, such as a football player, might very well be considered overweight and yet not have an excess of fat. The extra weight could be mostly muscle, which adds a lot to body weight. "Overfat" is the term used here to mean that the proportion of fat exceeds recognized established ideals. For men the ideal amount of fat is generally considered to be no more than 16 percent of body weight, and for women no more than 23 percent of body weight. By using this proportional measure, variations in body shape and size are taken into consideration.

*Height and Weight Charts*

Almost everyone is familiar with height and weight tables. They are frequently seen on "Weigh Yourself" scales and in many diet books. Height and weight tables are fast and easy to use and do give norms which can be generally useful in determining if you are under-or overweight for your height.

The major drawback to these tables is that they fail to take into account muscle and bone and can be misleading. An example occurred at one metropolitan police force which used height and weight tables as a standard for its members. The maximum allowable weight for a six-foot male was 210 pounds; above that weight an officer was considered overweight and subject to suspension. Two officers, both body builders, were six feet tall and over 210 pounds, but had only 9% and 10% fat as measured in other tests. While they may have been overweight for the normal person, they were certainly not overfat, which was the purpose of using the tables. Fortunately, after a lot of explanation about the difference between overweight and overfat, the officers were reinstated.

For the average American, the charts probably do reflect an indication of being overfat, so for a quick and easy reference height and weight charts do serve some purpose, but should not be overrated. There are charts in this book on pages 79 to 81.

You can also quickly do your own calculations.

Take your body weight in kilograms and add 100; take your height in centimeters; and then divide your height into your weight. The quotient should be right about 1. Over 1.1 is somewhat overweight, under .9 is underweight.

For accuracy, your weight should be measured on a medical balance-type scale rather than a spring-type scale. Spring scales can easily go out of whack.

*Skin Fold Measurement*

An accurate method for determining percentage of body fat is the taking of skin fold measurements. This is an entirely painless test which consists of "pinching" up a fold of skin at certain places on the body and then using calipers to measure the fold. Conversion tables are then used to determine the amount of fat versus lean tissue. This test is usually done prior to any tests involving exercise since holding onto dry skin is easier than holding onto sweaty skin and makes the measurements more accurate.

Usually three to six sites for measurement are used. For example, chest, thigh, above the hip, abdomen, triceps, and shoulder blade. The sum of these six points is used to get an average before using the conversion tables. As few as three sites may be used with accuracy. The measurements should be taken with metal calipers since they offer the greatest accuracy.

Taking the measurements requires experience and skill on the part of the tester. Any inaccuracies in the readings will result in inaccuracies in the conversion equations.

Since there is no practical way for average persons to perform this test on themselves, there is no need for any lengthy explanation of how the equations were determined, or to go into any detail of the conversion charts themselves. The resulting percentage of fat is all that really matters.

For men, acceptable range of fat is 16-23 percent; for women 23-28 percent. While not everyone can have an "ideal" shape and size, anyone can reach ideal percentage of fat—16 for men, 23 for women. It is possible for someone of either sex to be somewhat less fat than "ideal" without harmful consequences.

But just as too high a percentage of fat can be bad for you, so can too little fat. Men should not be less than 5 percent fat, nor women less than 12 percent fat. People who have too little fat are far less common than those who have too much, so there is usually only specialized concern given to underfat individuals and they are not dealt with in this book.

Do not be surprised if your tester takes and retakes the measurements at each site several times. This is done to get the most accurate reading and is a sign of experience rather than inexperience.

Women readers may be curious as to why their percent of fat is different from men. Women have what is known as "sexually specific" fat in breasts and hips. Allowance is made for the necessary fat in these areas, so women can more comfortably and attractively carry a higher percentage of fat than men.

Reducing the amount of fat can be done in two ways. One is the decrease of caloric intake and the other is an increase in the caloric expenditure. Even doing both of these at the same time still requires time to accomplish a reduction. Generally only two to three pounds of body weight can be lost safely per week. You should approach this reduction of fat as part of the overall fitness program and actually give more emphasis to the cardiovascular system over fat loss. Improving the C-V system will then enable you to perform the routines necessary to increase your calorie expenditure.

### Cardiovascular Endurance

Testing the cardiovascular system gives an accurate indication of the level of work at which you can safely perform without overtaxing the body. Your resting heart rate and resting blood pressure are used in these tests as a baseline for establishing how hard your body has to work to do a certain amount of exercise. From these tests it can be determined what types of exercise would be best for you, and how hard you should work at them. Remember that even if you start at a relatively elementary level that you will be working your way up to more strenuous exercise as your body adjusts.

The testing starts out usually with a simple step test and then may progress to running or a bike ergo-meter test.

### Step Test

The step test is very simple and requires only a 12-inch stool or bench as equipment. The test consists of having you step up onto the bench with one foot, then bring up the other foot, and then step down one foot at a time, and do this at a set rate for a set amount of time, usually 24 steps per minute for three minutes. At the end of the three-minute period the heart rate is taken and compared to established norms. The general indications are that the more fit a person is, the lower the heart rate at the end of this test. Since the work done is proportional to body weight, it is a good indication of the fitness of the cardiovascular system for a specific individual.

The modified Kasch step test is a standard for YMCAs and a chart of rates and norms is given on page 82. The results of the step test indicate at what level you can safely begin your program.

*Bicycle Ergometer Test*

The bicycle ergometer test, or bike test as it is often called, involves pedalling a special stationary bike which can be adjusted for the amount of resistance you must pedal against. This test can be used to estimate oxygen uptake (see page 83) and to predict your maximum workload so that a percentage of that workload can be used for your program.

The bike test uses low work rates to start. Then the heart rate is taken, and the next workload is set. With constant monitoring of the heart rate, individuals are guarded against overstressing.

Work is measured as mass x distance. The workloads are measured as mass x distance per a unit of time. The usual measurement is kilogram-meters per minute (KGM)—a kilogram-meter is the amount of work that you would have to do to lift one kilogram of weight (mass) one meter (distance) against the pull of gravity. This is a very exact measure and can be very accurately set on the ergometer.

Usually a man will begin with a setting of 300 KGM/min, and a woman with 150 KGM/min. The workload is then increased proportionally, to produce heart rates of between 110 to 140 beats per minute. If these heart rates and workloads are plotted out on a graph, it can be seen that the relationship is linear. The maximum heart rate and work load can be very accurately estimated without having to strain the participant to the maximum workload and maximum heart rate. Maximum heart rate is derived from the formula of 220 minus your age. In other words, a 40-year-old person should have a maximum heart rate of approximately 180 BPM.

Since the efficiency of the bike ergometer is relatively constant and known, the maximum oxygen uptake for any individual can also be estimated from this test by estimating his maximum workload. The aerobic capacity of an individual's body can then be defined and compared to existing standards to again determine where, in terms of fitness, that individual stands. Oxygen consumption per unit of body weight is an accurate measurement of fitness because it does take body size into consideration.

Maximum oxygen consumption is partly based on heredity—some people just have a high level and others have a lower level capacity. Training can improve the maximum oxygen consumption, but not to the extent of other areas.

Oxygen consumption is important in that it indicates the workload you can handle and therefore the ultimate physical fitness you can achieve. Training allows you to work at a higher percentage of your capacity, so it is again important to know what it is since a low oxygen consumption capacity may limit your potential.

Generally speaking, untrained people can only work at about 50 percent of their capacity while trained people can work at about 80 percent. Eventually, any increases in capacity will max out (reach a maximum) and increases will not show up on any tests. So, as you train and your running times get better, don't get discouraged if increases in oxygen uptake stop showing up.

The bike test is one of the most commonly used tests for cardiovascular fitness because it is very safe and the heart rate is constantly being monitored. The workload never exceeds 85 percent of the maximum and the predictions of maximum workload are accurate since the workload up to a certain point is actually known, not estimated.

In some places, a treadmill test may be used instead of the bike ergometer. Treadmills are not so accurate since they don't accurately measure a workload the way the bike test does. However, some Americans can walk or jog better than they can ride a bike and a bike can give local fatiguing of the leg muscles.

*Muscular Strength and Endurance*
Evaluating strength is a very difficult thing to do. Since, by definition, it is a single, most forceful con-

traction, it is not very safe to test, either. In many cases, grip strength is used as an evaluation since this is safe to test. In most cases, strength is measured by endurance. This usually involves using a fixed amount of weight and seeing how many repetitions of lifting or whatever can be done. Muscular endurance is tested by repeating an activity a number of times. These are classical measurements in fitness and have the test of time on their side.

There are about 22 major muscle groups in the body and it wouldn't be practical to test all of them separately to determine strength and endurance. Fortunately, it is possible to project overall body strength from a few tests such as sit-ups and bench press.

The sit-up test (see page 84) measures the strength and endurance of abdominal muscles. This muscle group is important not only for appearance, but also for good posture and maintaining the lower back. The test is usually conducted with a time limit since it is not always practical to have unlimited time to test how many sit-ups a person can actually do. The results are still accurate. Ideally, the sit-ups should be done with the legs bent and the feet not being held down. This truly measures the abdominals and rules out any use of hip flexors, but usually a compromise is made by holding the feet down and limiting the test to one minute.

A disadvantage of the sit-up test is that it may be a maximum exertion for some people. Some people may also try to hold their breath as they do the sit-ups and this is dangerous because it creates pressure in the chest cavity and can collapse the veins returning blood there, consequently reducing blood flow. To eliminate this you should either exhale or count out loud on each sit-up as you curl up.

The resulting number of sit-ups completed in the time alloted is then compared to existing norms. A low score indicates that you need to include more muscular endurance activities in your program, especially abdominal endurance.

Push-ups and pull-ups are other tests that may be used in this way. The problem with pull-ups is that some people can't lift their own body weight, so the bench press or curl is often used instead.

The bench press test (see page 85), as used in the YMCA fitness battery, is used to predict overall body strength. Don't try a bench press without a companion to "spot" the weight. It permits a fixed amount of weight to be used, rather than an amount proportional to body weight, so muscular endurance is tested. To do this test, participants lie supine on a bench and are then given a barbell with a fixed weight. Men usually are given 80 lbs. and women 35 lbs. Participants then press the weight up to full extension of the arms and then bring the bar down until it touches the chest. A metronome keeps cadence. There is no time limit in this test; the participants keep going until they can no longer keep cadence or can't press up. The results are then compared to norm tables. Again, a low score indicates a need for more strength and endurance exercises.

*Flexibility*

Just as testing all the muscle groups for strength and endurance is impractical, so is it impractical to test the flexibility of all the joints in the body. But again, a general flexibility test (see page 86) is used to indicate overall flexibility. Flexibility is important in reducing injury in exercise and other activities and is therefore important to overall fitness.

The standard test for flexbility is very simple. It is usually done at the end of a battery of testing because the body has had sufficient warm-up by that time. The individual being tested is seated on the floor or a mat, legs outstretched and flat on the floor (knees locked), and heels about 10 to 12 inches apart. A yardstick is placed between the legs with the 15-inch mark at the heels and the 1-inch mark toward the body. To measure flexibility the individual reaches with outstretched arms as far as possible down the yardstick and holds it for 2 or 3 seconds. The score is recorded in inches, with 15 being the acceptable level, but with some people able to reach beyond that.

An additional method of measuring flexibility is by using a protractor to actually measure the angles and range of motion which occur with the sitting and reaching flexibility test. There should be no bouncing to reach or bend farther—ballistics are not recommended for you anyway. Obviously a low score indicates the need for increasing your flexibility.

## Advanced Tests

You probably will not be exposed to, or even interested in, the advanced testing procedures. However, some of you may eventually work up to the point that you really get interested in these tests and will appreciate reading about them. Various groups, researchers, etc., may perform these tests which are not done for medical evaluation, but for very sophisticated physical evaluation.

The Graded Exercise Test (GXT) is sometimes used as a screening method by physicians for patients who may be entering a physical exercise program. It is done on a treadmill (or a bike can be used), often with an electrocardiogram hookup. The results can be converted to get cardio-vascular fitness values.

Underwater weighing has become popular with some people who are really concerned about measuring fat and body composition. It is a very tricky measurement which uses very sophisticated equipment and must be done in a laboratory setting. It is very sensitive to error, very time-consuming, and not really necessary for most people to learn what they want to know.

Muscle biopsy is sometimes used by athletes to indicate potential development, but again this is costly. Since nothing can really be changed, it is not practical for the general public. There are also machines which can measure strength and endurance of a muscle through sopohisticated plotting of force curves. This may be of interest to athletes, but not to general fitness participants.

## Summary

In summary, you should be aware that effective fitness testing can be done simply, accurately, and at low cost. The value in testing is that it helps you get into a program which is safe for you to undertake and it shows you where you are now, so you know where to begin. With results measured against established norms, you also have an idea of what your reasonable goals should be, but you may be able to exceed the norms in some areas.

The next chapter explains how to go about starting a fitness program.

# Height and Weight Chart

## Determining Frame Size
## Using Wrist Size in Inches

|  | Men | Women |
|---|---|---|
| *Small Frame* | 6 ½" or less | 5 ½" or less |
| *Medium Frame* | 6 ¾"—7 ¼" | 5 ¾" |
| *Large Frame* | 7 ½" or more | 6" or more |

# Height and Weight Chart

## Determination of "Desirable" Weight for Men*
### Weight in Pounds
### According to Frame (in Indoor Clothing)

| Height (without shoes) | | Small Frame | Medium Frame | Large Frame |
|---|---|---|---|---|
| *Feet* | *Inches* | | | |
| 5 | 1 | 112-120 | 118-129 | 126-141 |
| 5 | 2 | 115-123 | 121-133 | 129-144 |
| 5 | 3 | 118-126 | 124-136 | 132-148 |
| 5 | 4 | 121-129 | 127-139 | 135-152 |
| 5 | 5 | 124-133 | 130-143 | 138-156 |
| 5 | 6 | 128-137 | 134-147 | 142-161 |
| 5 | 7 | 132-141 | 138-152 | 147-166 |
| 5 | 8 | 136-145 | 142-156 | 151-170 |
| 5 | 9 | 140-150 | 146-160 | 155-174 |
| 5 | 10 | 144-154 | 150-165 | 159-179 |
| 5 | 11 | 148-158 | 154-170 | 164-184 |
| 6 | 0 | 152-162 | 158-175 | 168-189 |
| 6 | 1 | 156-167 | 162-180 | 173-194 |
| 6 | 2 | 160-171 | 167-185 | 178-199 |
| 6 | 3 | 164-175 | 172-190 | 182-204 |

*Tables adapted from those provided as a courtesy by the Metropolitan Life Insurance Company

# Height and Weight Chart

## Determination of "Desirable" Weight for Women*
### Weight in Pounds
### According to Frame (in Indoor Clothing)

| Height (without shoes) | | Small Frame | Medium Frame | Large Frame |
|---|---|---|---|---|
| Feet | Inches | | | |
| 4 | 8 | 92-98 | 96-107 | 104-119 |
| 4 | 9 | 94-101 | 98-110 | 106-122 |
| 4 | 10 | 96-104 | 101-113 | 109-125 |
| 4 | 11 | 99-107 | 104-116 | 112-128 |
| 5 | 0 | 102-110 | 107-119 | 115-131 |
| 5 | 1 | 105-113 | 110-122 | 118-134 |
| 5 | 2 | 108-116 | 113-126 | 121-138 |
| 5 | 3 | 111-119 | 116-130 | 125-142 |
| 5 | 4 | 114-123 | 120-135 | 129-146 |
| 5 | 5 | 118-127 | 124-139 | 133-150 |
| 5 | 6 | 122-131 | 128-143 | 137-154 |
| 5 | 7 | 126-135 | 132-147 | 141-158 |
| 5 | 8 | 130-140 | 136-151 | 145-163 |
| 5 | 9 | 134-144 | 140-155 | 149-168 |
| 5 | 10 | 138-148 | 144-159 | 153-173 |

*Tables adapted from those provided as a courtesy of the Metropolitan Life Insurance Company

# Kasch—Three Minute Step Test Norms

| Rating | Heart Rate | |
| --- | --- | --- |
| | Males | Females |
| *Excellent* | 75-80 | 77-82 |
| *Good* | 85-90 | 88-93 |
| *Average* | 95-115 | 99-119 |
| *Fair* | 120-125 | 125-130 |
| *Poor* | 130-135 | 135-140 |

# Oxygen Uptake Test

| Rating | 35 and Under Males ml/kg | 35 and Under Females ml/kg | 36-45 Years Males ml/kg | 36-45 Years Females ml/kg | 46 and Over Males ml/kg | 46 and Over Females ml/kg |
|---|---|---|---|---|---|---|
| Excellent | 54 | 55 | 53 | 49 | 43 | 46 |
| Good | 49 | 45 | 45 | 43 | 38 | 38 |
| Above Aver. | 46 | 39 | 39 | 37 | 34 | 32 |
| Average | 36 | 34 | 33 | 33 | 30 | 27 |
| Below Aver. | 32 | 30 | 29 | 29 | 27 | 24 |
| Fair | 28 | 26 | 25 | 26 | 24 | 20 |
| Poor | 24 | 20 | 23 | 22 | 20 | 18 |

# Sit Up Test

| Rating | 35 and Under Males | 35 and Under Females | 36-45 Years Males | 36-45 Years Females | 46 and Over Males | 46 and Over Females |
|---|---|---|---|---|---|---|
| | *Repetitions in One Minute* | | | | | |
| *Excellent* | 45 | 39 | 42 | 39 | 38 | 24 |
| *Good* | 41 | 34 | 38 | 29 | 33 | 20 |
| *Above Aver.* | 37 | 30 | 32 | 22 | 26 | 17 |
| *Average* | 33 | 25 | 27 | 18 | 21 | 14 |
| *Below Aver.* | 28 | 20 | 21 | 12 | 18 | 11 |
| *Fair* | 23 | 15 | 18 | 9 | 15 | 7 |
| *Poor* | 18 | 10 | 11 | 4 | 10 | 2 |

# Bench Press Test

| Rating | 35 and Under | | 36–45 Years | | 46 and Over | |
|---|---|---|---|---|---|---|
| | Males | Females | Males | Females | Males | Females |
| | *Number of Repetitions* | | | | | |
| *Excellent* | 35 | 30 | 30 | 29 | 28 | 30 |
| *Good* | 29 | 24 | 24 | 21 | 22 | 22 |
| *Above Aver.* | 24 | 20 | 19 | 18 | 19 | 18 |
| *Average* | 20 | 16 | 17 | 15 | 16 | 14 |
| *Below Aver.* | 15 | 13 | 14 | 11 | 12 | 9 |
| *Fair* | 11 | 10 | 10 | 7 | 8 | 5 |
| *Poor* | 7 | 5 | 3 | 4 | 3 | 2 |

# Flexability Test

| Rating | 35 and Under | | 36–45 Years | | 46 and Over | |
|---|---|---|---|---|---|---|
| | Males | Females | Males | Females | Males | Females |
| *Trunk Flex (in Inches)* | | | | | | |
| *Excellent* | 21 | 23 | 22 | 23 | 20 | 22 |
| *Good* | 19 | 21 | 19 | 21 | 17 | 19 |
| *Above Aver.* | 17 | 20 | 16 | 19 | 15 | 18 |
| *Average* | 15 | 18 | 14 | 17 | 13 | 15 |
| *Below Aver.* | 12 | 15 | 12 | 14 | 11 | 14 |
| *Fair* | 9 | 14 | 10 | 12 | 8 | 11 |
| *Poor* | 7 | 11 | 5 | 10 | 5 | 9 |

# 6. Starting the Program

The moment of truth is now at hand. You've learned about the commitment it is going to take to get into shape and about how your body works in reaction to the program you are about to begin. And you've found out where you are now so you can realistically begin a program and set goals. Now you must start the program.

## Getting Started

To begin, you must have a set of goals and ideas about how you expect to achieve them. Your long-term goal will undoubtedly be overall fitness, so you will be concentrating on reaching that through a series of short-term goals. Write down your ultimate goals (remember these may change later), such as being able to run two miles and feel good about it, do 30 sit-ups in two minutes, weigh X amount, wear size x slacks or dress, etc. Then work backwards to set your short-term goals. You may want to start with your immediate goals first, and then fill in the other spaces later.

Your immediate goals will depend a lot on your evaluation testing and where you can begin. If a walking program with limited calesthetics is your starting point, your goals might be to walk 15 minutes at a brisk pace each day and to perform x number of calisthenic activities. If you are in better shape to start, your goals will be more ambitious.

No matter what shape you are in, if you haven't been exercising regularly you should start slowly and not try to progress too fast. If you go too fast, you will get sore, tired, and frustrated, all of which will hamper your enthusiasm for your program. You must balance your activities so that they match your abilities and don't discourage your continued commitment. Once you have found a comfortable level of activity, stick with it for one or two weeks before you think about increasing the level. After this initial period, increase what you are doing by 5 to 10 percent.

This rate of increase is called progression, which is a vital key to your success. You want to start off at a level that is relatively comfortable, but difficult enough that you know you are working. You want to be able to say to yourself quickly, "Hey, this is easy, let's try something harder", and keep your enthusiasm high as you move up. A steady, graduated progression will give you the benefit of increased work without overstress and discouragement. Don't try to take quantum leaps from level to level. Keep it smooth and easy.

# How to Train Effectively

How you do your activities is just as important as what activities you do. Effective training is based on three factors: frequency, duration, and intensity.

Frequency is how often you exercise. The best schedule is to do your fitness program every other day, or at least three times a week. If you are really enthusiastic you could do your program up to six days a week, but beyond that there is no real benefit. Seven days of the same routine may be harmful for you. Your chances of becoming injured increase and you greatly increase your chances of becoming bored with the whole thing. For the seventh day you should change your activity to informal sports or games —something that is not so demanding as your usual routine.

Duration is how long you exercise each time. A minimum of 20 minutes each time, at 60% of the maximum heart rate (see next section on intensity), is needed to achieve a training effect. Less than 15 minutes won't do you much good. The longer you exercise the more you will get out of it, but there is a maximum. Exercising for one hour is not twice so beneficial as exercising for one-half hour, so don't kill yourself. Twenty to 30 minutes each time is perfectly adequate.

Intensity is how hard you work, measured by your heart rate. You can work too hard if you don't know how to control the intensity of a work-out. If you have to strain, the intensity is too high. Again, if the intensity is too high, you may get discouraged.

To control the level of intensity you use heart rate as a guide. You estimate your maximum heart rate by using the figure 220 and then subtracting your age. This is your maximum heart rate and you should be training at a level of 60 to 80 percent of your maximum; 60 percent for beginners, 80 percent for highly trained individuals.

Using a percentage of maximum heart rate is the easiest and safest way to regulate intensity because it is automatically regulated by your own fitness level. For example, if you are 40 years old, your maximum heart rate would be 180 and 70% of that (your training rate) would be 126. Simply choose an activity which produces that rate for you. A beginner in a program may find that 126 is produced from brisk walking, while better conditioned people may find that they have to jog to get up to 126. As fitness increases, so does the level of intensity you have to reach in order to get to your maximum heart rate percentage. It's very simple, self-regulating, self-progressing method. Later on, as your fitness increases, you can increase the percentage of your maximum heart rate you use as a training rate.

Another method used to determine a training rate is called the Karvonan system. This sytem subtracts the resting heart rate from the maximum heart rate and then uses a range of 60% to 85% as the training range. The resulting range is similar to maximum heart rate minus your age. However, the Karvonan system is considered more individualized and more sophisticated.

## The Three Phases of Training

No matter what activities you are doing in your program, there are three phases you must go through: warm up, intense training, and cool down. Warm-up is the period just before your training when you do a few exercises to raise your body temperature and limber your body. The reason for a warm-up period is that it "gets the juices flowing" in terms of readiness for your training and helps reduce the likelihood of injury.

The intense training period is when you do your cardiovascular exercises, your activities for muscular strength and endurance, and whatever other exercises you choose. This is the 20-minute (minimum) period of true training.

Cool down is the transition period from intense training to your everyday activities. You are returning your body to the resting state. A rule of thumb for this is that when your heart rate slows to 100 beats per minute, you are sufficiently cooled down. The cool-down period usually involves doing a few easy exercises for flexibility. Cool down means not having a sudden stop in movement until your heart rate is 100.

## The Order of Training

Fitness participants often question whether it makes any difference which activity they do first. Should they start with cardiovascular activities or muscular strength activities? The order is not important, but the first activity naturally gets the best effort from you and therefore you should do first whatever it is you need or want to concentrate on most. Overall, your training period would be five to ten minutes of warm-up, 20 to 30 minutes of intense training, and then five to 10 minutes of cool down. Those people who are better trained will warm up and cool down faster than beginners.

*The Importance of a Training Routine*

Establishing a training routine is important to your continued success. Setting aside a set period every day or every other day for your activities and sticking to it will make it a natural part of your life. You should make this time period and the method of training as easy on yourself as possible.

If you are someone who hates morning, don't set it up so that you have to rise at 5 a.m. to do your daily dozen. That's self-defeating and you'll soon drop out of your own program. If you are going to go to a fitness facility such as the local YMCA, plan to go on your lunch hour or your way home, or some way that it is easy for you to do it. The location, the timing, and how all this matches up with your "buddy" and his or her plans will take some adjustments at first. If it doesn't become second nature, (like going to church on Sunday morning), chances are you won't stick with it.

If you are in an organized program, chances are that a record card for your activities and progression will be provided. If not, or if you are on your own, start one yourself. You should record the date (frequency), the length of time you worked out (duration), and the activities and their times or repetitions (intensity). If working with weights, record the weight and number of repetitions for each set. For running, record distances and time. These records will both show your progress and give you benchmarks when you may be ready to increase the activity again. Always record your heart rate at the end of the intense training period. This is your indicator of whether or not the activity is right for you or if you should increase the intensity. A good digital watch is easiest to use for counting the heart rate, but there is no reason to invest in one just for this purpose. If you are interested in losing weight, your daily weight can be recorded in the same log.

*Equipment Needed for Training*

There is no need to spend a great deal of money on equipment for fitness training. A minimum investment in clothing for shorts, top, warmup, socks and shoes will see you through most activities. For some, such as swimming and racquet sports, the purchase of eye-protective goggles is strongly recommended. For running and jogging, a good pair of shoes is a wise investment. They may seem expensive (more than a pair of street shoes), but they will last for lots of miles. When you consider that three to six times your own weight is transferred through the foot when you jog, a good pair is well worth it. If you aren't sure how to choose the best shoes for your type of activity, ask at a reputable sports store for an explanation of what is best and why.

One of the real benefits of true fitness training is that it is inexpensive, really requiring only a few dollars to be done right—plus your time and commitment.

*Using Training Machines*
If you are in a program or at a facility which offers resistance machines or weights, be sure to get professional advice from the instructors on how to use this equipment properly. Some of the new equipment is very sophisticated and might cause injury if not used properly.

The same goes for calisthentics you might perform there or at home. Be sure you know how to do them correctly and that you are doing them for the right reasons. Injury is always a possibility, but its chances are lessened when you know the how and why of what you are doing.

*Training for Muscular Strength and Endurance*
Training for muscular conditioning should be done with a moderate amount of repetitions with minimum resistance. This will do the most for you for overall conditioning.

Training for muscular strength is done with high resistance, hundreds of pounds of weight, and low repetitions, perhaps three to five.

Training for endurance is just the opposite: low resistance and a very high number of repetitions.

Choose a weight which allows you to do about ten to 20 repetitions. If you can't do ten you are using too much weight, while if you can do more than 20 you may not be using enough weight. Again, this is for overall fitness; if you have special goals in mind, like big biceps, your activities and levels will differ from this general plan.

It is the usual practice in fitness training to do two to three sets, or series of repetitions, of one exercise. There is no clear-cut rest period between them. You may wish to plan your workout so that you go from one activity to another and then repeat the cycle for your second, and then third, set of repetitions. This way you rest a particular muscle group in between repetitions, but you don't waste time by resting and doing nothing. You should also plan your workout so that you work alternate groups of muscles and achieve a balance rather than overworking one group.

*Training for Flexibility*

Exercises done to increase flexibility are best done when the muscles are warmed up. For this reason it is recommended that flexibility training exercises be done after cardiovascular and strength and endurance activities. Joints should be worked through their full range of motion and you should stretch to a position, hold it for a few seconds, and then relax the position. Do not bounce, it is counterproductive. Again, work alternative groups so that the effect is balanced and one group is not overworked.

Individuals who are below normal in flexibility may want to do stretching exercises more frequently than just during their workout periods. You can do these exercises up to four times a day. You might follow a schedule of stretching right after you get up in the morning, then doing them before and after other exercises (warm up/cool down), and again just before going to bed. Flexibility exercises are also a good way to relieve soreness and pain which may be a result of your other program activities. If you have attained normal flexibility or have adjusted to your routine so that soreness is not a big problem, you can cut back flexibility exercises to just during your normal exercise routine.

## What to Expect from Training

The truth of the matter is that you shouldn't expect too much, too soon. Training is a long, slow process, especially if you have neglected it for years. Training will benefit all areas of the body and these improvements will show up as you progress. Some of the improvements may not be outwardly apparent, such as an improved heart rate, so record keeping is important if you really want to see your overall progress.

One of the most important things as you begin fitness training is to establish the proper behavior patterns and techniques. If you lay the firm foundation for fitness, it will stay with you for the rest of your life. You might compare it to playing the piano. About everyone starts at the same place, practicing scales, developing techniques, and so on, and eventually piano playing becomes second nature. No one plays the piano well without practicing, and no one remains fit without training. The results will come if you stick with it, so stick with it.

# 7. Starting Your Own Program of Fitness

Even in an organized fitness program, your activities and outlook must be totally your own. No one else is exactly where you are or has the same goals and attitudes. It is extremely important to realize this because the major tendency is to compare yourself to others and their training. Human nature being what it is, we don't compare ourselves to those who are starting at a lower level than we are. Instead we look around and see only those who are doing more than we are. If you must look at those people and compare them to yourself, think of their level as a goal you are striving to reach. Chances are they started where you are now, so that should provide an incentive for you.

Your goals (both long-term and short-term) should be well thought out at this point. The short-term ones are the progressive steps you are planning to take and the long-term goal is the sum of all those steps.

## Personal Considerations

Since this is your program of fitness, it must be an acceptable program to you, even pleasurable if possible. So if it is suggested that you walk two miles a day and you can't stand the thought of it, do something else. There are alternatives to every exercise. Choose the ones that give you the most satisfaction, as long as you choose a fitness activity and not just something that is fun to do. Dancing (of some types), swimming, cycling, tennis, and many others, can all be fitness activities if they are pursued in that light and done regularly. There is no reason to jog around a boring indoor track if you don't like it. However, bowling, for example, is not an activity which contributes appreciably to any increase in fitness. In fact, its social nature may be counterproductive by encouraging you to drink and eat foods which aren't in your best fitness interests. This is not to say you shouldn't go bowling. Just don't go bowling thinking that it is part of your fitness activities.

*Time*

"But I don't have any time" is a comment frequently heard as an excuse for not taking up a fitness program. While you may feel that all your waking moments are already allotted, chances are that you really can squeeze in the 30 to 45 minutes needed to perform fitness training. Most people are unaware of how much time they really waste and yet they somehow find time to watch that football game on TV or the first 30 minutes of the late movie.

If you can't consistently set aside 30 minutes or

more three times a week, you will not succeed at a fitness program.

By scheduling your fitness training over the lunch hour, or after or before work, you may actually find that you are increasing your productivity in the time you do your regular work and that you are cutting down on overeating, a second bonus to your fitness. For those who argue that they really do have too much else to do, the answer is that by taking the time to get fit they will probably live longer, happier, more productive lives. Therefore, they will actually be able to get more done in the long run by taking time for fitness now. Lack of time, the most common excuse, is probably the weakest excuse for not training.

*Scheduling*

You must create a regular time and place for your fitness training. Again, this is a very personal choice and may mean a weird schedule of doing it at midnight or 4 a.m., at home or at an organized facility. You may decide to bicycle to work, or jog to the train, or walk up ten flights of stairs to your office, all in the name of your fitness. But you have to do it regularly. No time of day is better than any other and no one activity is without its alternatives.

## Facilities and Equipment

Done correctly and planned well, your fitness program can readily adjust to the equipment and facilities to which you have the easiest access and can comfortably afford. If swimming is part of your plan, then you must have access to a pool. If you don't, you should choose an alternate exercise.

Expenses can vary from the minimal investment in a pair of jogging shoes to hundreds or thousands of dollars a year to join a health club facility. You need only spend what you want to.

## Support Groups

As mentioned previously, a support group or buddy of some kind is important to keep you going. While this may not be essential after your routine is firmly established, it is very important in the beginning. Friends, family, or strangers who share a fitness interest can form your support. In addition to keeping you committed to your program, a support system allows you to share problems and reduce the daily stress you may feel. Stress management is another area of overall health and fitness, so this should be of concern to you, too.

## Self-Evaluation

As your fitness improves you should be upgrading your activities to keep methodically increasing the work you are doing. If you are in an organized program which provided pretesting, you can always ask for an annual retest to quantify your improvements. If you were tested at a private testing facility you have the same option. Retesting more frequently than annually is not really necessary, and the improvement levels may not be significant enough to give you the boost you expect.

On a month-to-month basis you should be able

objectively to assess your improvement by your increase in workload or ease of doing a current workload and by the review of the careful records you've been keeping (see Chapter Six section on "The Importance of a Training Routine").

For runners, joggers, and walkers, timing yourself over a set distance is one way of measuring your progress. For other activities such as weight lifting, you can use weight and number of repetitions. For swimming you can either measure a certain distance (or laps) in time or just count any increase in laps you are able to swim. There's always a way for individuals to self-test to gauge their improvements. If you stick with your program, there will be improvements to measure.

# 8. Your Long-Term Plans

Use your imagination a little right now. Imagine that you have been doing your fitness training program for several years now, you are in good overall health, your weight is well controlled, you feel great, and you simply want to maintain this level of fitness without becoming a fanatic about it. What do you do now? You don't want to give up all you have accomplished, but the prospect of running those same miles, or doing those same exercises is just too boring to consider.

The answer is simple, and you may not even have this problem if you have been thinking about your long-term plans: you adjust your activities to your personal needs.

Successful long-term planning for fitness is centered around three key factors: goals, enjoyment, and variety. If you have reached your major long-term goal of overall fitness, you may simply change this to a lifetime goal of maintaining this level. A maintenance program requires less time and work than the building-up process, so you are freed for other activities that still promote fitness.

Enjoyment is key. While your commitment to fitness may have been a large part of keeping you going even when the going got tedious, you now need something that will keep you going because you enjoy it and it is healthful.

It can't be said more perfectly than in the old phrase, "variety is the spice of life". That applies to fitness activities most appropriately. Since variety of activities can fulfill your fitness needs and your enjoyment goals at the same time. Having a variety of interests is most important.

Long-term planning (which doesn't necessarily mean that you have this all neatly planned out in advance, only that you are aware of the need) is important because in a few years you will not be the same person, living the same life, you are now. Age changes us. Perhaps hang gliding no longer holds the thrill and attraction it did a few years ago. Or you may move from Wisconsin to Florida and cross-country skiing becomes impractical. You may get married or have children and family activities have to be integrated into yours. You need to be prepared to make changes in your fitness program for all the changes that can and will occur.

We repeat that you should select new activities which you enjoy. You may want to test some activities to see if you enjoy them before making any commitment. You may find that some you were sure you would enjoy, you don't. Be flexible and sensible.

When starting any new activity you will have to make physical adjustments. If you are in good overall condition, you don't have to start at the lowest level, but you should still approach any new activity with some caution. If you switch from swimming to cycling, expect soreness in the legs. You'll work into a new activity faster than a poorly-conditioned novice, but you will still have to work into it. Just as you used a slow progression in your fitness program, you should do the same with new activities. Fortunately the progression should be much faster.

One of the real pleasures of taking up new activities is the acquiring of new skills which may open the way to additional activities and interests. Also, you will no doubt meet many new people. This adds to your enjoyment. An added benefit to having a variety of activities is that it expands your options if an injury occurs which limits your regular fitness program. Injuries will occur to everyone, so don't think it won't happen to you. A sprained wrist may keep you from playing tennis, but it might not keep you from jogging or cycling. Be prepared by having a variety of activities.

If you have been successful and pleased with your fitness program, you will of course want to encourage your friends to do the same. The best way to do this is by example, not by becoming an evangelistic browbeater. You can actually come across to others as too fit and too well ("healthier than thou") if all you ever do is talk about that one subject and end up turning everyone else away from it. Set an example and invite your friends to join you in an activity they would enjoy. Properly led by example, many of your friends will see the benefits of fitness and join you without any pushing at all.

Your overall, long-term goals, therefore become fitness at all ages and for all ages. Your choice of eating sensibly, exercising, and having a variety of interests, will automatically be passed on to your children, too, so it even extends to the next generation. For yourself, long-term planning will enable you to maintain your fitness throughout your life, no matter where you live and no matter what activities are available to you. As we stated at the beginning of this book, fitness is a lifetime commitment and one that will give you a lifetime of pleasure.

# 9. Fitness Activities For You

The purpose of this chapter is to give you a list of activities which can be used as part of a fitness program and to point out the advantages and disadvantages of each. Again, a variety of activities will keep up your interest in fitness and provide you with alternatives when you need them. The descriptions here are brief, but books have been written on every one of them. If you have a particular interest, go to the library or bookstore and read more.

## Walking

Walking, meaning brisk walking, is probably the most underrated fitness activity there is. Its advantages are: it provides good cardiovascular exercise; it is a very low stress activity; it can be done virtually anywhere; and it can be done by people of all ages. Its major disadvantages are that it is difficult to get a high level of training with walking and that it requires more time than other activities, such as jogging or running, to be beneficial.

## Jogging and Running

Jogging and running are the two most popular fitness activities today. They are a very fast way to burn up calories and give good cardiovascular training. Another advantage is that jogging and running are currently a very social thing to do, so it is usually easy to find someone with whom you can do it. The disadvantages are that it is a high stress activity and injuries are common.

## Swimming

Swimming is good exercise in that it exercises all the muscle groups, is non-weight-bearing and has a low stress level. The disadvantages are that swimming requires special skills, a pool, and another person to watch (a lifeguard.)

## Bicycling

Biking is a very entertaining activity. It is easy to do and has a low stress level. It does require a special skill and is often limited by weather. Indoor biking (exercycle type) doesn't have the scenic value and can be expensive, but isn't limited by weather.

## Cross-Country Skiing

Cross-country skiing can be a great deal of fun to do and it gives a high level of training, by using most of the body. An added advantage is that it is less weight bearing than running or jogging. The major disadvantages are that it is limited seasonally and requires specialized skill and expensive equipment.

## Racquet Sports

Included here are racquetball, tennis, squash, and paddleball. These sports have the advantages of improving agility, giving some cardiovascular training, and involving many parts of the body. The major drawbacks are the need of a partner and specialized facilities and equipment. You can learn the closed court sports faster than tennis.

## Basketball/Volleyball

These court sports give good cardiovascular training, add to agility and coordination, and do involve the the use of many parts of the body. The major drawbacks are the need for a team of players and special skills, equipment, and a special playing area.

## Weight Training

Weight training is an excellent way to make gains in muscular strength and endurance, but it has very limited cardiovascular effect. Other drawbacks are that it is stressful and requires specialized equipment and facilities which can be expensive.

## Aerobic Dancing

Aerobic dancing is very popular today, mainly because it is so much fun to do. It provides excellent cardiovascular training. Good programs also incorporate flexibility and muscular strength and endurance training as well. This activity also provides excellent group support. The disadvantages are that it requires an instructor and music and may need a large area to accommodate the group.

## Skating

Ice skating and roller skating provide good leg exercise and a high training level. The stress factor is low, but special skills and special equipment and facilities are needed.

## Calisthenics

The major advantage of calisthenics is that they require no equipment to develop muscular strength and conditioning.

# 10. Fitness Checklist

☐ Get a friend to join you on this journey.
☐ Set short-term goals.
☐ Set long-term goals.
☐ Take one thing at a time and progress in short steps.

Check your:
☐ Current level of fitness.
☐ Resting heart rate.
☐ Resting blood pressure.
☐ Body composition.
☐ Cardiovascular endurance.
☐ Muscular strength, endurance, and flexibility.
☐ Current patterns of living.
☐ Time for exercising.
☐ Available exercise sites.

Increase your knowledge about your own body:
☐ The interrelations of your systems.
☐ Body composition.
☐ Control of accumulated fat.
☐ Muscular conditioning and flexibility.

- [ ] Workload increases and heart conditioning.
- [ ] Maintainence of well-balanced diet.
- [ ] Age and Environment.
- [ ] Establish and maintain frequency, duration and intensity.
- [ ] Always warm-up before intense training and cool-down afterward.
- [ ] Start workload low and increase slowly.
- [ ] Work entire muscle completely.

Do Not:
- [ ] Exercise on a hit-or-miss basis.
- [ ] Bounce muscles while exercising.
- [ ] Overbend your back backwards.
- [ ] Bend your knees sideways.
- [ ] Put too much pressure on neck muscles.
- [ ] Lift too much weight and overstrain your back.
- [ ] Expect too much too soon.

Make it fun:
- [ ] Choose things you enjoy doing.
- [ ] Evaluate progress each month and set new goals.
- [ ] Vary your exercise activities to keep things interesting.
- [ ] Support that friend who works out with you and together get another person to join you!

Stay fit!

# Index

# Index

## A

Abdominal, 74
Advanced tests, 76
Aerobic dance, 109
Age, 46-47
All or none, 53
Altitude, 48, 49

## B

Ballistic(s), 55, 76
Basketball, 109
Bench press, 75, 85
Bicycle(ing), 22, 108
Bicycle ergometer, 70, 71-73
Blood pressure, 39, 62, 64
Body composition, 32, 61, 65, 77
Body fat, 43, 68
Body structure, 32
Body type, 32
Bone, 36
Bouncing, 55
Bowling, 98

## C

Calisthenics, 110

Caloric expenditure, 70
Caloric intake, 69
Calories, 34, 37, 42, 45
Cardiovascular, 31, 37, 61, 70, 91
Cholesterol, 38
Chronic diseases (illness), 63
Cold, 48, 49
Commitment, 21
Conduction, 48
Connective tissue, 36
Convection, 48
Cool-down, 91, 92, 95
Cross-country skiing, 108

## D

Dance(ing), 98
Diastolic, 39, 65
Diet, 23, 43
Duration, 89, 92

## E

Electrocardiogram (EKG), 77
Emotional fitness, 18
Endurance, 36, 47